Shropshire Railways Pictorial

compiled and edited by the

Shropshire Railway Society

Shropshire Books

ACKNOWLEDGEMENTS

The Shropshire Railway Society are greatly indebted to the following photographers for permission to include their work in this book:
Geoffrey Bannister, Michael Embrey, David Giddins, Horace Mapp, Russell Mulford, E. M. Neale, L. N. Owen, Berwyn Stevens, Graham Vincent, Peter Ward, Derek Whalley, "The Herefordshire Times" and "Real Photos".

Special thanks must also go to the following society members who have been responsible for collating the information and photographs in this collection:
Keith Davies, Michael Embrey, David Giddins, John Massey and Berwyn Stevens. They were assisted in this task by Len Davies, John Humphreys, Russell Mulford and Steve Price.

Front cover picture:
One of Bristol's allocation of Hawksworth-built GW Hall 4.6.0's No 6981 'Marbury Hall' tackles the long southbound climb out of Shrewsbury with a West of England express during the exceptionally severe winter of 1962/3.

Back cover picture:
Careworn, but faithful to the end, Hudswell-Clarke 0.6.0T 1587 'Unity' lifts another load of coal from Ifton Colliery sidings on 29th October 1968, just two weeks before the mine was closed. View from the driver's side looking down the branch line towards Preesgweene.

ISBN 0-903802-42-2 ©Shropshire Railway Society 1989
Cover and book design: Sarah Barker
Published by Shropshire Books, Shropshire Leisure Services, Preston Street, Shrewsbury
Printed in Great Britain by Adams & Sons (Printers) Ltd, Hereford

British Library Cataloguing in Publication Data
Shropshire railways pictorial
1. England, Shropshire, Railways, History
I. Shropshire Railway Society
385'.09424'5

SHROPSHIRE RAILWAYS — A WARM MEMORY

As a child, living just over the border in Staffordshire, I used to think that Shropshire was the place where small and rather insignificant trains came from, to be lengthened and furnished with dining cars and bigger engines at Wolverhampton and thus turned into proper expresses befitting their continuance to Paddington. When I got to know Shropshire better I soon learned how wrong I had been. Of the nine routes meeting in Shrewsbury the one to Wolverhampton ranked almost as a branch. It is true that some of the trains that went on to there had come from Chester or Birkenhead but even with an ultimate destination like the metropolis, the Shrewsbury people regarded them as small fry compared with the great 'North-and-West' Expresses that came thundering down from Crewe behind some of the most powerful engines the LMS could find and afterwards tackled the ups and downs of the Hereford line, often heroically pulled by GWR engines of seemingly smaller proportions.

Some had come from Manchester; some from as far afield as Glasgow and Edinburgh (from which they supplied the bookstall with the latest editions of 'The Scotsman'). Some went on to Cardiff; others to Kingswear to give a Torbay tan to palefaced, raindrenched Mancunians—and some as far as the ultimate bufferstops at Penzance. In either direction they always had an aura of true rail travel that eclipsed the Paddington-Birkenhead expresses on the GWR line.

But Shropshire could offer many different railway delights, indeed it is doubtful whether any other county had such a variety, and this is splendidly represented in the following pages. This second selection to be compiled by members of the Shropshire Railway Society is not intended as a history of our lines, that is available elsewhere—but in these pages the reader will find more facets of our railway past than any history could display.

This is not a book of train pictures of the kind that might have been taken anywhere. These photographs demonstrate the character of local railways—and enthusiasts might say they even had a personality. In some it was rougish, awkward, occasionally belligerent too— yet frequently lovable at the same time. It was often a case of 'travelling hopefully' and many of the minor lines like the 'Potts', the Bishops Castle, the Snailbeach and the Cleobury Mortimer and Ditton Priors teetered on the brink of closure for years before they actually folded. Some survived just long enough to rise temporarily to new heights to serve their country in time of war, while others carried on until the dreaded 'Beeching Axe' fell remorselessly upon their tracks, their bridges and their stations.

Now we regret their precipitate demise. More and more people are turning to the railways to get away from the horrors of road congestion. New, fast and comfortable services are dramatically raising receipts. Stations are reopening and there are calls to reopen lines too. Unfortunately most were obliterated beyond the point of recall so that never again will we see those tiny, inoffensive mineral branches that despite their unobtrusive presence in the landscape, carried tonnage of stone and other goods that wreak such havoc in the country-lane-lorry-loads of today. The picture of youngsters joy riding on the Cothercott Mining Company line may appear as light relief, but such lines could serve remote quarries where no lorry could reach without costly and destructive roadmaking of a totally unacceptable nature and thus the photo also highlights a more serious change in circumstances.

For years Shropshire played host to the tiniest of all standard gauge locomotives, the East Anglian-born 'Gazelle'. What a delight to see it here, gently simmering on its branch. There is even a genuine 'Duke'—so very much more elegant than their rebuilt successors drawn from cannibalized 'Dukes' and 'Bulldogs'. The hilly nature of much of the terrain is recalled on the one hand by a view of almost the only bit of main line flat enough to locate watertroughs, while on the other a splendid pair of photos show the old and new cars on Britain's only inland cliff lift at Bridgnorth. For some strange reason these are otherwise confined to the seaside, and the extremities of this contrivance, together with the headquarters of the Severn Valley Railway, allow the town to claim no less than three stations, none of which belong to British Rail! A fine miniature railway operated on the Hilton Valley and this is now relocated in another part of the country. Some of these railways survive, but others like the 'Coalport Dodger', Kinnerley and Buildwas Junctions and the great Coleham sheds can only remain in memory and in photograph—and how much the one is helped by the other.

We are proud of our railway heritage in Shropshire.

We have already reversed the trend for closures and where British Rail can no longer hope to operate, others have stepped in to preserve the memory. The Severn Valley Railway does this in a practical manner; the Cambrian Railway Society keeps alive the memory of the great railway works and headquarters at Oswestry and has future hopes for services, while as we go to press there are proposals for some commemoration of the 'Potts' in new developments on its site in Shrewsbury. All these and other schemes, together with everyone interested in railways, will be indebted to the mine of information so fascinatingly revealed in this collection of photographs.

by John Horsley Denton,
President of the Shropshire Railway Society, author of 'Ghost Trains of Shropshire' (BBC), 'Shrewsbury Railway Station' and many other publications.

Shropshire Railways Pictorial

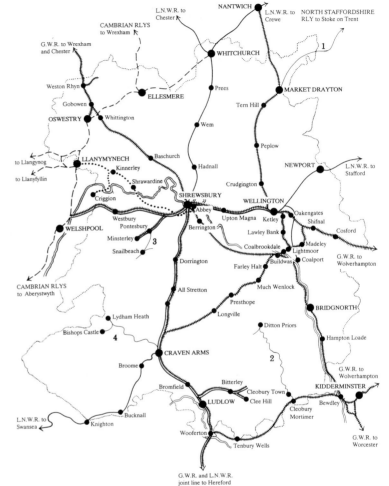

CAMBRIAN RLYS to Wrexham

L.N.W.R. to Chester

NANTWICH

L.N.W.R. to Crewe

NORTH STAFFORDSHIRE RLY to Stoke on Trent

1

G.W.R. to Wrexham and Chester

WHITCHURCH

MARKET DRAYTON

Weston Rhyn

Prees

ELLESMERE

Gobowen

Tern Hill

OSWESTRY

Whittington

Wem

Peplow

NEWPORT

L.N.W.R. to Stafford

to Llangynog

LLANYMYNECH

Baschurch

Kinnerley

Hadnall

to Llanyfyllin

Shrawardine

Crudgington

Criggion

SHREWSBURY

WELLINGTON

Oakengates

Abbey

Upton Magna

Ketley

Shifnal

WELSHPOOL

Westbury

Pontesbury

Berrington

Lawley Bank

Cosford

Minsterley

3

Coalbrookdale

Madeley

Lightmoor

Snailbeach

Buildwas

Coalport

G.W.R. to Wolverhampton

Dorrington

Farley Halt

CAMBRIAN RLYS to Aberystwyth

All Stretton

Much Wenlock

Presthope

BRIDGNORTH

Longville

Ditton Priors

Lydham Heath

2

Hampton Loade

Bishops Castle

4

G.W.R. to Wolverhampton

CRAVEN ARMS

Broome

Bitterley

KIDDERMINSTER

Bromfield

Cleobury Town

Clee Hill

Bewdley

LUDLOW

Cleobury Mortimer

L.N.W.R. to Swansea

Bucknall

Knighton

Wooferton

G.W.R. to Worcester

Tenbury Wells

G.W.R. and L.N.W.R. joint line to Hereford

╫╫╫╫╫╫ Great Western Railways

────── London North Western Railways

── ── ── Cambrian Railways

• • • • • Shropshire and Montgomeryshire Railways

──── Minor Lines 1 North Staffordshire Railway

2 Cleobury Mortimer and Ditton Priors Railway

3 Snailbeach District Railway

4 Bishops Castle Railway

Under the covered roof at the south end of Shrewsbury Station in the mid-1950's stands No 1000 'County of Middlesex', on a Birkenhead to Paddington express. No 1000 of Chester (84k) was the first 1945 County Class built at Swindon by the Great Western Railway. On Platform 7 is an express from Liverpool (Lime St) to the West of England. At this time Shrewsbury was a mecca for train spotters.

The overhead footbridge, frames an ex-LMS Patriot, at the south end of Shrewsbury Station in 1952. The bridge was demolished in 1960 when the station was modernised.

An atmospheric scene in the contrasting light and shade as Castle Class No 5091 'Cleeve Abbey' with a full head of steam waits to depart. It has just been attached to the Manchester to Plymouth express. This was a typical scene at Shrewsbury in the mid-1950's when the overall roof was still in position.

Patriot Class No 45507 'Royal Tank Corps' departs with an express from the south of England, bound for Manchester. The locomotive is on a running in turn after an overhaul at Crewe works, and eventually will return to its home depot of Carlisle (Upperby). It would have been attached at Shrewsbury and would probably only work the train as far as Crewe.

This picture shows how busy Shrewsbury Station was in the 1950's. The three ex-LMS locomotives at the northern end are all ready to depart. From left to right, 41159 one of the famous Midland Compounds, 42935 a Horwich Crab which was allocated to Nuneaton (2B), and on the right, 45548 'Lytham St Anne's' a Patriot class allocated to Carnforth (24L). The cast bridge in the foreground was replaced in 1962 by a steel bridge, still there today.

5

A sad sight as one of the main roof supports is lowered onto Platform 3 at Shrewsbury Station. Demolition of the roof was started in 1961 and completed the following year.

6028 'King George VI' photographed in 1960. The crew replenish the tender from the water crane at the north end of Shrewsbury's Platform 4. It has just brought in the Cambrian Coast express from Paddington.

Displaying a Machynlleth shed code plate, BR Standard Class 4MT Number 80098 waits at Platform 1 with the local All Stations to Aberystwyth service in the early 1960's.

A West of England, Bristol to Crewe express enters Shrewsbury in 1955, hauled by LM Patriot Class 45536 'Private W Wood, VC'. This locomotive was one of the pre-war Patriot Class engines rebuilt in 1946 and given a tapered boiler and double chimney at the LMS Crewe Works.

Shrewsbury LMS shed staff photographed just after nationalisation in 1948. Behind them is an LMS Black 5, with its first BR number M4748. Left to right: Bob Langstaff (fitters apprentice), Charlie Davies (fitters apprentice), John Skitt (boilersmiths apprentice), Bill Preece (fitters apprentice), Bert Duckworth (coppersmith), George Canham (fitters apprentice), Charlie Booth (fitter), Reg Worrall (fitters mate), Tom Price (fitters mate), Arthur Johnson (fitters mate), Charlie Morris (labourer).

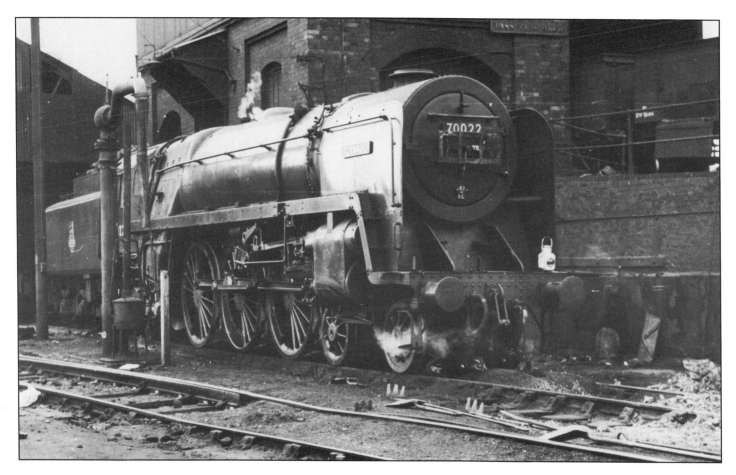

A rare visitor to Shrewbury, Newton Abbot based 70022 'Tornado' is serviced on the Great Western Shed at Coleham. It would then be returned to its home shed. These locomotives were thoroughly disliked by the Devon crews, and by 1957 fifteen were reallocated to Cardiff Canton, so they became more common on the North and West route.

Midland Compound 41159 on the turntable at Shrewsbury LMS shed in 1957. These famous engines were introduced by Johnson in 1902, developed by Deeley and Fowler and brought to their final stage in LMS days. They were one of the most successful British compound designs with a driving wheel diameter of 6'9" and a tractive effort of 22,649 lbs. Note the old grounded coach behind 41159 which was used as a working hut.

Stanier Black 5 No 45116 is prepared for her passenger working to Chester on Saturday 4th March 1967. This engine was in charge of the last steam passenger train running from Shrewsbury on Sunday evening to Chester.

Former LMS 2.6.0 Locomotive No 42964, a Stanier Mogul, stands on the shed at Shrewsbury in 1956. The engine was allocated to Crewe South (5B). The class was introduced in 1933 with a tapered boiler, 5'6" driving wheels and a tractive effort of 26,290 lbs.

GWR 4.6.0. King Class Locomotive No 6010 'King Charles I' stands in Shrewsbury shed in the summer sunshine of 1961. The engine was allocated to Old Oak Common (81A). The signal box was used for movements on shed and on the main line.

The great days of steam are captured in this 1950's scene on Shrewbury shed. Four locomotives from left to right are Patriot Class 45543 allocated to Manchester Longsight (9A), Black Five 44768 allocated to Liverpool, Edge Hill (8A), 8F Class 48474 allocated to Shrewsbury (84G) and Standard 5MT 73093 also of 84G.

A shed scene at Shrewsbury during 1959. The Castle Class 5061 'Earl of Birkenhead' (84K) Chester allocation, has just arrived from Chester. On the right stands modified Hall Class No 6980 'Llanrumney Hall' allocated to Shrewsbury (84G) and two other GWR unidentified locomotives. The footpath on the righthand side of the picture, known as Rocke Walk, was a regular spotting area for local railway enthusiasts during the steam era.

Activity at Sutton Bridge Junction in the mid-1950's: A BR Standard Class 5 passes the signal box with a southbound freight train. Meanwhile, GWR 0.6.0 Pannier Tank No 3782 carries out shunting duties in Coleham Yard. In the background a fireman trims the coal in the tender of a Stanier-built locomotive, and various locomotives can be seen on the shed area beyond.

A Western Region, Swindon-built, cross country diesel multiple unit approaches Sutton Bridge signal box on a special service during 1960. A very busy background scene with both former LMS and GWR engines in steam. In the foreground a water column with the old gasometer dominating the skyline.

An empty coaching stock train returning from Bridgnorth in the 1960's after working a special RAF diagram, passes Sutton Bridge signal box and joins the main line into Shrewsbury. The locomotive is a GWR 4300 Class 2.6.0 No 7338, allocated to Worcester Shed (85A). A fine wooden bracket signal can be seen behind the signal box.

A 1953 photograph of a GWR 0.6.0 pannier tank locomotive pausing at Sutton Bridge signal box with the 10.42 from Bewdley. The fireman hands over the token for the single line section from Berrington to Sutton Bridge. This appears to be quite a stretch for the signalman. In the background is Coleham Goods Yard to the left of the Hereford main line. The building on the extreme right is the railway clearing house with a paraffin storage hut in front.

A GWR 4.4.0 No 3440 'City of Truro' coming up to Sutton Bridge Junction and heading south with a returning excursion from Crewe to Cardiff on 27th May 1958. Seen two days earlier in Penzance, this much travelled locomotive was allegedly the first to reach 100 mph. It achieved this feat in 1904 when travelling down Wellington Bank, south of Taunton. In 1930 it was in the old York Railway Museum. Reprieved in 1957 it was restored to working order at Swindon but banished to Swindon's GWR Museum in 1962. The Severn Valley Railway at Bridgnorth claimed it in 1984 and restored it for the GWR 150 years celebrations. 'City of Truro' can now be seen at the National Railway Museum at York.

Approaching Sutton Bridge Junction in the early 1950's is a Dukedog Class No 9005 pulling a mixed freight from its home depot, Machynlleth, and destined for Coleham Yard.

Two locomotives in 1952 at Sutton Bridge both displaying a Hereford shed code (85C). GWR Saint Class No 2920 'Saint David' is held on the up line at signals, while GWR Mogul Class No 6326 waits in the loop with a loaded cement slab train. The two train crews can be seen discussing the hold up. In the background there are numerous wagons on what is known locally as the 'shelf sidings'.

GWR 4.6.0 Castle Class Locomotive No 5001 'Llandovery Castle' passes under the Shropshire and Montgomery Light Railway bridge near Belle Vue, Shrewsbury in 1950. The train is a Manchester to Cardiff express. A northbound freight train is seen held in the loop at Sutton Bridge. Engine No 5001 was allocated to Cardiff Canton (86C).

War Department austerity tank engine number 125 on the daily goods run at Shrewsbury's Abbey Station in 1959. The line was run by the WD Civilian Division from 1947 until 29th February 1960, and from 31st March 1960 handed over to BR (WR), and the Shrewsbury end was re-joined onto the Severn Valley line.

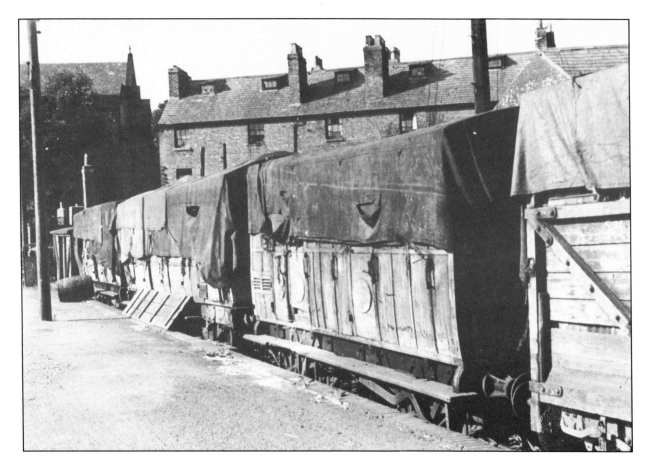

A line of old Shropshire and Montgomeryshire Railway coaches, vans and cattle trucks in the bay platform of Shrewsbury Abbey Station. They were used for storage until scrapped in 1952.

A GWR Manor Class No 7827 'Lydham Manor' working empty stock passes Meole Brace in 1964. The Shrewsbury West "Potts" interchange sidings were on the left side of the fence beyond the footbridge.

28

Two Dukedogs 9004 and 9014 double-head a Talyllyn Railway special train bound for Tywyn on 26th September 1959. Both the 4.4.0 Class 9000 locomotives were allocated to Machynlleth (89C). The special is passing Meole Brace. The Shropshire and Montgomery Light Railway track can be seen alongside the main line and the A5 trunk road crosses the picture at right-angles in the background. This was the final train to be hauled by these veterans, and after the return working, both engines were put into store on Wellington shed.

The only locomotive of its class built by British Rail at Crewe in 1954, Standard Pacific No 71000 'Duke of Gloucester' makes an impressive sight climbing Crewe Bank. The locomotive is pulling an express from the West of England bound for Manchester on 6th August 1954. Due to its excessive appetite for coal, and constant problems with the Caprotti valve gear, the locomotive was reduced to second link workings such as parcel duties, and was finally withdrawn in November 1962. It languished in Barry scrapyard for almost eleven years before it was purchased for £4,950 by a group of enthusiasts. It has now been restored to full working order by the Great Central Railway at Loughborough.

Former GWR 2.6.0 Mogul No 5331 allocated to Shrewsbury (84G) heads a permanent way spoil train away from a deep dig on Crewe Bank during 1954. The locomotive is working wrong road passing the Sentinel Wagon Works with a considerable load of clay in the open wagons. Another open wagon can be seen in the works yard, which in those days had a rail connection. A GWR pannier tank made a daily visit on weekdays conveying goods to and from the factory.

British Railways standard 3MT 2.6.2 Tank No 82002 allocated to Chester West (6E) heads towards Wellington in the early spring sunshine of April 1959. The photograph was taken at Belvidere Bridge. The train is the 12.20 from Shrewsbury to Stafford.

Shrewsbury's locomotive depot at Coleham on a March night in 1965. Eight 4.6.0 locomotives stand outside the LMS shed: an ex-LM Jubilee and a Black 5, Standard Class 5 and 4, and four ex-GW manors. 7822 'Foxcote Manor', in the foreground is about to leave to work a freight for Oxley (Wolverhampton), whilst on the right, 7812 'Erlstoke Manor' has its fire dropped, after working in from Aberystwyth on the evening mail.

After the last seven Manors were withdrawn in November 1965, Shrewsbury's allocation of Standard Class 4.6.0's handled all the steam workings on the Mid-Wales route. This picture, taken in December 1966 shows double chimneyed 75029 climbing vigorously out of Shrewsbury, past the site of the S & MR interchange yard with the afternoon down Cambrian Coast express.

Ex-GWR mixed traffic 4.6.0 No 7819 'Hinton Manor' climbs away from Hookagate signal box, where the crew have just collected the single line token to Hanwood. 7819 is working the down Cambrian Coast express on 26th September 1964.

The NCB-owned tank locomotive at Ifton Colliery, near St Martins, in 1967. This colliery had a private three mile long branch line to Preesgweene on the Shrewsbury-Chester main line. For more than forty years the coal traffic was handled by this Hudswell-Clarke 0.6.OT No 1587 'Unity'. She was supplied new in 1927 to the colliery owners, W Y Craig & Sons Ltd. The NCB closed the mine in November 1968, and 'Unity' found a new home at Harrington Pit, near Workington, Cumbria.

Track maintenance work is being carried out on the Shrewsbury to Wellington line between Belvidere Bridge and Upton Magna Station.

A GWR 4.6.0 Manor class locomotive is in attendance standing in the winter sunshine of 1960.

A GWR Castle Class No 7000 'Viscount Portal' heads an early morning Liverpool to West of England express past Shrewsbury Golf Club at Meole Brace in the early 1950's. A heavy freight train working from South Wales is held in the loop waiting to enter the Sutton Bridge section.

Former GWR 4.6.0 No 7019 'Fowey Castle' steaming up the gradient towards Bayston Hill with the 13.30 Shrewsbury to Bristol express in March 1953. The locomotive was allocated to Bristol Bath Road (82A). Kemp's Eye footbridge can be seen in the background.

8F 2.8.0 No 48434 on a Central Wales freight run, southbound at All Stretton on 31st December 1960.

Two ex-LMS 2.6.4 Fowler Tanks Nos 42385 and 42387 are seen approaching Bayley's Bridge, near Bayston Hill with a Shrewsbury to Swansea Victoria service returning to Swansea on 19th June 1958. To overcome the arduous climb on the Central Wales line double-heading was quite a common practice on this service.

In the mid-1950's a Hereford Mogul No 6330 returns home assisting a modified Hall class locomotive on the long climb towards Church Stretton. The train is seen here passing Dorrington Station.

An Abergavenny Bowen Cooke LNW 0.8.0, photographed in 1954, on a mixed freight run from Shrewsbury to the Severn Tunnel Junction. It is seen here returning south through Church Stretton Station.

A photograph taken in 1954 showing a Stanier 8F No 48739 with a northbound freight train as it trundles past the beautifully kept Church Stretton Station, bedecked with hanging flower baskets and spotless signs and notice boards. The GWR-designed station buildings were demolished in February 1970, and replaced by a structure resembling a bus shelter. The original railway station is a listed building and still stands to the north of the road bridge.

On 6th June 1955 an old war horse chugs down the easy gradient past Little Stretton halt, seen in the background beyond the bridge. Built from Robinson's Great Central Railway design in 1917 for the Army Railway Operating Division, a number of engines were taken into GWR stock in 1919 and fitted with Great Western boilers. No 3041 was not withdrawn from service until 1957.

A WR Cross Country 3-Car diesel multiple unit (DMU) pauses briefly at Craven Arms on its journey from Shrewsbury to Cardiff General. A pannier tank is shunting on the down siding between the platform and the signal box. These attractive buildings were, regrettably, demolished in 1970.

A pair of exiles languish on Craven Arms shed in 1956. One of the last surviving LNW Coal Tanks No 58904 is buffered up to a Johnson Midland 2F 0.6.0 (probably 58213). Both locomotives were in store, unlikely to run again.

At Bromfield on 1st April 1953, an ex-GWR 0.6.0 No 2274 with a southbound freight overran catch points on the north side of the station and demolished the buffer stop. Fortunately, both footplate crew escaped with only minor injuries and both lines were cleared by five p.m.

The only watertroughs in Shropshire were located north of Ludlow, near the racecourse. A Cardiff (Canton) allocated Brittania Class No 70027 'Rising Star' replenishes its water supply as it speeds southbound in the late 1950's with a Manchester to Cardiff General express.

The scene of the Ludlow collision on 6th September 1956. At two o'clock in the morning the North and West main up line in the Ludlow area was blocked by a lorry which collided with the level crossing gates at Bromfield. As a result, single line working was in operation and the 16.45 Penzance-Crewe express headed by Ex-LMS Jubilee Class No 45644 Howe was brought to a standstill at signals north of the station. The following 14.00 parcels train from Penzance to Crewe headed by GWR Mogul No 9306 ran through a red signal and collided with the rear of the stationary express. Luckily the rear of the express, consisting of a bogie milk van and brake, absorbed the force of the impact and the rest of the train was little harmed. The only casualities were two passengers who suffered shock.

A 2.6.2T No 4401 pulling a Wellington to Craven Arms train through Rushbury in April 1951, not long before the withdrawal of passenger services from Much Wenlock to Craven Arms. The station building is now a private house.

In the shadow of the now demolished Buildwas "A" power station stands a single car DMU at the platform for Much Wenlock in the summer of 1961. The Wellington, Buildwas to Much Wenlock line closed on 23rd July 1962.

(a)

(b)

On Saturday 23rd April 1955, the Stephenson Locomotive Society, North Westen Area, and the Manchester Locomotive Society held their tenth tour called 'The Shropshire Railtour'. The train was pulled by an ex-GWR Dean 0.6.0 No 2516. The tour departed from Shrewsbury at 14.30, to travel via Wellington to the Much Wenlock branch and forward to Longville. It returned from Longville along the closed section from Lightmoor Junction to Madeley Junction, then along another closed section, the ex-LNW branch from Hadley to Coalport. Next it returned to Wellington and on to Shrewsbury taking the Abbey Foregate loop to avoid the station and reach the ex-LNW and GW branch line to Minsterley. It finally returned to Shrewsbury at 19.50 hrs. The total distance covered was about one hundred miles, and the tour cost 15s 6d.

Three photographs of the 'Railtour' taken at:

(a) Farley Halt on the section from Buildwas to Much Wenlock which closed completely on 23rd July 1962.

(b) Beyond Much Wenlock at Presthope on the line to Marsh Farm Junction which closed on 31st December 1951.

(c) Coming off the Coalbrookdale line at Madeley Junction. The scene has changed today: a new signal box has been built in the Junction, and the land on either side of the line is clothed with Telford's new factory units.

(c)

(a)

(b)

(c)

(a) Three miles along the main line from Wellington was Lawley Bank, between Ketley Junction and Lightmoor, with combined signal cabin and shelter by the level crossing. It was opened for goods traffic in 1859, and passengers in 1960. It was then closed completely from 23rd July 1962.

(b) 7817 'Garsington Manor' passes through Wellington on a non-stop summer Saturday express in the early sixties. The train is probably the 7.10 Pwhelli to Paddington.

(c) Castle Class No 5034 'Corfe Castle' displaying a Reading shed code plate (81D) is seen here approaching Wellington with the 8.56 Ramsgate-Birkenhead express in June 1958.

(a)

(b)

(c)

(a) Wellington, a sub shed of Wolverhampton, was a small three road structure of uncertain date and origin. In 1950 the allocation here was 24 locomotives, of which not more than six could be housed at any one time. Class 2MT No 41204, and GWR Class 0.6.0 Pannier Tank No 3732 are awaiting their next duties. The shed was finally demolished in August 1964.

(b) LNWR 0.6.0 Coal Tank No 58904 at Coalport East on 15th July 1950 pulling a Wellington train. The line opened on 17th June 1851 and passenger services ceased here on 2nd June 1951. The Great Western station on the Severn Valley line was on the opposite side of the river.

(c) On 15th July 1950 an LNWR 0.6.2 Coal Tank No 58904 waits to depart from Newport to Wellington. Three hundred of this type of locomotive were built at Crewe between 1881 and 1896. The line between Wellington and Stafford closed for passenger service on 5th October 1964.

(a)

(b)

(a) New Hadley Halt, between Wellington and Oakengates, opened in 1941. It was moved from its original position where it was built in the early 1930's. The halt finally closed on 11th May 1985.

(b) Shifnal Station in 1955. This station was originally opened by the Shrewsbury and Birmingham Railway Company in 1849.

This photograph of the Hilton Valley Railway, then near Bridgnorth, was taken in the mid-1960's. On the left is 2.6.0 No 2 'Teddy' built by T N Liversage of Herne Bay in 1950. It ran on the Herne Bay Pier Railway for one year and came to Hilton in 1964. The locomotive on the right was No 3, a 4.8.4 built at the F H Lloyd Training School in 1959, under the supervision of Mr T F Naylor, and named after the Founder of the company, 'Francis Henry Lloyd'. The railway is now based at Weston Park.

The Bridgnorth Cliff Railway was opened in July 1892. It had two carriages built by Metropolitan Vickers, mounted on steel girders, each housing a 2,000 gallon water tank which was filled at the top station from a 30,000 gallon water tank on top of the station roof. When full it weighed 9 tons, which was enough to raise the carriage and a maximum of 18 passengers. When it reached the bottom, the water was emptied out and pumped up to the storage tank. The process was then repeated. In April 1933 the railway closed, but in May 1934 it was re-opened by a new company. In December 1944 the hydraulic operation was converted to electric winding and air brakes were fitted.

In 1955 the cars were replaced by an improved streamlined design with better heating and lighting. The railway has the double distinction of being the only inland cliff railway and having the steepest and shortest incline with a 1 in 1.5 gradient.

Opened 19th July 1908, Cleobury Town Station on the Cleobury Mortimer and Ditton Priors Railway in Admirality ownership, before goods traffic ceased 16th April 1965. The concrete station on the left came from the nearby Abdon Quarry Company in 1919, and contained the CMDDR offices. On the right stood the Burwarton Coal and Trading Company shed and a weighbridge. The last passenger train ran in GW days on 24th September 1938. The line was taken over from BR (WR) by the Admirality on 1st May 1957.

(a)

(b)

(c)

Two photographs taken on the Severn Valley line in 1954 at Hampton Loade.

(a) A W19W GW Diesel Railcar waits with a local Bridgnorth to Kidderminster service. This batch of railcars were built at Swindon in 1940 and carried 48 passengers.

(b) Pannier Tank No 8718 returns to Kidderminster with a local pick up of freight from Bridgnorth. Passenger and freight traffic on this line ceased in late 1963, but returned in May 1970 when the Severn Valley Railway Society received legal authority to operate trains between Bridgnorth and Hampton Loade.

SIGNAL BOXES

(c) The Dorrington Signal Box on the Shrewsbury to Hereford railway line is one of five S & H boxes still intact.

(a)

(b)

(c)

SIGNAL BOXES

(a) This GW box at Crudgington closed with the line on 9th September 1963. The line opened as the Wellington and Market Drayton Railway on 16th October 1867.

(b) Berrington's GW box in March 1968, ten days before demolition. It closed with the Severn Valley line on 9th September 1963.

(c) The modern BR Wellington No 2 Box was commissioned in May 1952 to replace a wooden North Western Box.

A very orderly Kinnerley Station, photographed when closing in March 1960. The S & M main line to Llanymynech heads west to the top right of the picture, whilst the Criggion branch curves away to the left past the locomotive shed. The buildings still survive today.

(a)

(b)

(c)

(a) A Birmingham Loco Club Special on the Shropshire and Montgomery Railway on 26th June 1955 on Shrawardine Viaduct. The locomotive is an army Hunslet 0.6.0 ST No 193, now preserved at Llangollen. The first two coaches were built for the London Tilbury and Southend Railway, and used on the Ealing to Southend through service. The viaduct was dismantled in 1962 after the line was closed in March 1960.

(b) S & MR 0.4.2WT 'Gazelle' at Llanymynech in 1938. Built by Dodmans of Kings Lynn in 1893, originally as a 2.2.2WT, it is now housed at the Army Transport Museum at Beverley. The carriage behind was originally one of the Wolseley Siddeley railcars built in 1923. It was scrapped in 1935 and converted to the trailer for 'Gazelle' in 1936.

(c) This Sentinel No 7026 four-wheeled locomotive built in 1927 for the British Quarrying Company has a vertical boiler. It is seen here shunting on the Criggion sidings at the end of the Shropshire and Montgomery line. This part of the line, which was used for quarry traffic from 1929 to 1959, ran for a mile in a south-westerly direction, along the foot of a steep escarpment in the Breidden Hills. Halfway along the line was a crushing plant and sidings for wagons waiting to be filled at the crusher. The Sentinel locomotive was scrapped on site by J Rollason of Wellington in April 1962.

Standard Class 2MT No 78005 stands in Llanymynech Station in 1959. The train is an Oswestry to Welshpool mixed freight. Llanymynech was a scene of great activity at this time. In the main yard on the left, condemned wagons were broken up. The famous Shropshire and Montgomery Light Railway on the right was used for storing condemned rolling stock before it was broken up. The bay platform on the left side was originally for the Llanyfyllin branch line trains which would run in the bay, engine first, to the buffers. Access to the branch was gained by reversing to a head shunt (out of picture) and climbing the embankment seen on the far left in the background. Note the platform steps seen in the lower left foreground which illustrate a common Cambrian Railway hazard: lower platforms.

Standard Class 4MT 4.6.0 Locomotive No 75026, a native of Machynlleth (89C), stands at Llanymynech Station on Saturday 16th January 1965. The train is the 12.15 local passenger service from Welshpool to Oswestry. Two days after this photograph was taken, the line from Whitchurch to Buttington Junction was closed.

Ivatt 2MT 2.6.0 Locomotive No 46509 (89A) stands in its home station of Owestry during April 1959. The train is the Oswestry to Llanfyllin mid-day down local service. The general practice was for the locomotive to work tender first towards Llanfyllin then return to Oswestry the correct way round.

Oswestry shed was the largest depot of the Cambrian Railways and was set in the fork of the lines to Gobowen and Whitchurch. On 31st December 1947, 36 engines were allocated to this depot. This photograph, taken in the mid-1950's, shows an assortment of locomotives: two GWR Pannier Tanks, GWR Dean goods, LMS Ivatt Mogul, GWR Collet goods, and another GWR Dean goods. In January 1965 Oswestry sheds and station were closed.

(a)

(b)

(c)

(a) The view from the north end of Oswestry's up platform in the winter of 1948. The middle foreground is dominated by the huge footbridge which gave access to the carriage, wagon and locomotive works. Attempts have been made recently to secure the preservation of the footbridge as a tribute to Oswestry's railway heritage. The amount of traffic handled by the station in its heyday is very evident in this photograph. Note also the original Cambrian signal arms on the gantry in the foreground.

(b) A GWR 4.4.0 Duke Class No 9054 'Cornubia' stands outside Oswestry shed in August 1949. This locomotive was built in July 1895 and was originally numbered 3254. The eleven engines renumbered in the 90XX series all passed into BR stock, and this particular engine recorded the highest mileage of the class, 1,632,815 miles, before its withdrawal in June 1950.

(c) Oswestry Works in 1960, showing an ex-Cambrian Railway belt-driven wheel lathe.

(a)

(b)

(c)

(a) Shrewsbury based Jubilee 45572 'Eire', an unlikely visitor inside Oswestry Works in 1962, receiving attention to its side rod bearings during a mileage overhaul.

(b) Inside the Oswestry wagon repair shop in 1960, showing the drop forge on the left.

(c) An ex-GWR Castle Class No 5061 'Earl of Birkenhead' coupled to a Hawksworth 4000 gallon slab-sided tender is seen pulling into Gobowen Station in the mid-1950's with a local service from Chester to Shrewsbury. The engine was withdrawn in September 1962 having travelled over one million miles.

𝔓𝔥𝔬𝔱𝔬𝔤𝔯𝔞𝔭𝔥𝔦𝔠 𝔖𝔬𝔲𝔳𝔢𝔫𝔦𝔯

in connection with the

LAST TRAIN

on the

SHROPSHIRE and MONTGOMERYSHIRE RAILWAY

SUNDAY, 20th MARCH, 1960

Organised by

THE STEPHENSON LOCOMOTIVE SOCIETY

(Midland Area)

Chronology of the line

Potteries, Shrewsbury and North Wales Railway o. 13th August, 1866, cl. 21st December, 1866, re-opened December, 1868, closed and abandoned as from 22nd June, 1880.

Re-opened as Shropshire and Montgomeryshire Railway on 13th Apl. 1911, (Criggion branch on 21st February, 1912).

Passenger services ceased from 6th November, 1933.

Government control assumed as from September, 1939.

1941—ma'n line (Shrewsbury-L'anymynech) requisitioned by WD.

1947—WD Military status to WD Civilian status.

1948—become part of B.R.—the Railway Executive, Western Region. (Only the Criggion branch was affected by this).

1959—Military depots closed and tracks lifted. Criggion branch closed completely after cessation of quarry traffic in December.

1960—29th February, civilian rail traffic facilities ceased; the last train actually worked from Abbey station, Shrewsbury, on 26th February, when work commenced upon a connection from Abbey goods yard to the Severn Valley branch of the W.R. From this date the outlet for military traffic became Llanymynech.

As soon as all W.D. equipment has been removed the line will be formally handed back to B.R. (W.R.)—dismantling will follow.

BRITISH RAILWAYS
WESTERN REGION

Oldwoods Halt
Stanwardine Halt
Haughton Halt

WEEKDAYS ONLY

UNTIL FURTHER NOTICE, PASSENGER TRAINS WILL CALL AT THESE HALTS ON WEEKDAYS AT THE TIMES SHEWN BELOW :—

DOWN TRAINS

For GOBOWEN, OSWESTRY, WREXHAM, etc.

		a.m.	p.m.	p.m.	p.m.
			WEEK-DAYS.		
OLDWOODS HALT	dep.	7.55	1.56	5. 1	6.57
STANWARDINE HALT	,,	8. 4	2. 5	5.11	7. 7
HAUGHTON HALT	,,	8. 9	2.11	5.17	7S12

UP TRAINS

For SHREWSBURY, etc.

		a.m.	p.m.	p.m.	p.m.
			WEEK-DAYS.		
HAUGHTON HALT	dep.	8.45	12S40	—	6.27
STANWARDINE HALT	,,	8.51	12S46	—	—
OLDWOODS HALT	,,	9. 0	12S57	3. 9	—

S—Saturdays only.

September, 1956.

(25) Ch. 12. H.   PRINTED IN ENGLAND BY JOSEPH WONES LTD.   WEST BROMWICH.   (H)

(a)

(b)

(c)

(a) BR Standard Class 4 No 76044 passes through Wem Station in the early 1960's with an engineering train full of soiled ballast bound for Gresty Lane, Crewe. The centre portion of the footbridge was left without a roof to allow the signals to be seen in either direction by the approaching train drivers. Today the station still remains open, but the footbridge and station buildings have long since been demolished.

(b) Dukedog 4.4.0 No 9020 standing on the Whitchurch shed. This was an LNWR shed which housed the Cambrian Line engines from Oswestry. In the last week of 1947 GW locomotive 7819 'Hinton Manor' was officially allocated here. The shed was opened in 1863, became a sub-shed to Crewe North (5A) after nationalisation in 1948, and was closed in 1957.

(c) Peplow Station was the second station from Wellington on the Nantwich line. At the time this photograph was taken in 1960 the station still had a small goods service. Peplow, like others on the line, closed on 9th September 1963.

(a)

(b)

(a) Tern Hill Station photographed in 1960 looking towards Market
   Drayton. The station closed on 9th September 1963 as part of the
   Beeching cuts. The bridge in the background carries the main A41
   trunk road. The platforms and station buildings were demolished
   along with the track but some remains are still evident today.

Market Drayton Station taken in 1958:

(b) Looking east towards Silverdale Junction. The building on the
   right is of GWR origin, while the building on the left was built
   by the North Staffordshire Railway Company.

(c) The main public entrance to the GWR Station.
   At Silverdale Junction the North Staffordshire line from Stoke-
   on-Trent joined the main Wellington to Crewe line, and trains
   from the Potteries ran to the station until 1952. The line was finally
   closed on 9th September 1963. The goods shed and offices still
   remain and are used by North Shropshire District Council as an
   office and depot.

(c)

One of the two locomotives Nos 3 & 4, 4.6.0 side tanks, built by the Baldwin Loco Company of America for use on the 60 cm gauge lines in France during the First World War. They were built of rugged construction so they could be used on hastily laid, uneven track. In 1918 they were rebuilt by Messrs Bagnalls, with WD numbers 538 and 722 (Works Nos 44383 of 1916 and 44572 of 1918). In 1923 they commenced work on the Snailbeach District Railway. Their livery was black with the SDR Nos painted on the buffer beams in white. They worked all the traffic up to the end of steam working in July 1946 and were finally cut up on site in May 1950.

Youngsters joyriding on the Cothercott Mining Company line south of Pulverbatch. It was a 1′10 ¾″ gauge railway system with steeply graded tramway. The locomotive which worked it, 'Minstrel Park', built by Hunslett in 1877, was formerly at Dinorwic Quarry, and came to this line in the 1920's. The track was removed in 1946.